The Show Must Go On

Fond Memories of Cee Hill
And
Glimpses of the Life of the
Howard Gunter Clan

Heather Gunter Campbell

by

Heather Gunter Campbell

Printed in Victoria, Canada

National Library of Canada Cataloguing in Publication Data

Campbell, Heather Gunter, 1940-
      The show must go on / Heather Gunter Campbell.

ISBN 1-55395-794-6

      1. Wollaston (Ont.)--History--Anecdotes. 2. Campbell, Heather Gunter, 1940- --Family--Anecdotes. I. Title.

FC3099.W652C34 2003   971.3'585   C2003-900802-9
F1059.W62C34 2003

TRAFFORD

This book was published *on-demand* in cooperation with Trafford Publishing.
On-demand publishing is a unique process and service of making a book available for retail sale to the public taking advantage of on-demand manufacturing and Internet marketing.
On-demand publishing includes promotions, retail sales, manufacturing, order fulfilment, accounting and collecting royalties on behalf of the author.

Suite 6E, 2333 Government St., Victoria, B.C. V8T 4P4, CANADA

Phone	250-383-6864	Toll-free 1-888-232-4444 (Canada & US)
Fax	250-383-6804	E-mail sales@trafford.com
Web site	www.trafford.com	TRAFFORD PUBLISHING IS A DIVISION OF TRAFFORD HOLDINGS LTD.
Trafford Catalogue #03-0157		www.trafford.com/robots/03-0157.html

10   9   8   7   6   5   4   3   2   1

CONTENTS

Dedication

I humbly dedicate this book to Mom, in memory of Dad. Dad's stories were my motivation for writing, but Mom and Dad were a team for the biggest share of Dad's eighty-seven years.

Mom was always the photographer in the family and many of the pictures in this book are snapshots that she took over the years. Thanks to her good organization, the photos were labelled and assembled in albums.

I also want to thank Aunt Madge King, Dad's sister, for some of the older pictures and for her help in some of the *history details*. I am sorry that there is not enough space to list all the names of others who have helped as this book was taking shape. I have tried for accuracy and apologize if there are any incorrect interpretations.

A big thank you goes to Patricia Elford of my Writers' Club for her editing and proofreading skills and to Elizabeth Warren and Maureen Gunter who also helped with the proofreading. I thank them too, as well as many other family members and friends, for their encouragement.

I take full responsibility for any structural errors since I did make minor changes after the proofreading.

Major gratitude is extended to Frank, my long-suffering and patient husband, who has been my computer technician. I doubt that I would have been able to complete this book without him.

Foreword

I am fascinated with the weekly 'Antique Roadshow' seen each week on television. Because of it, I find myself admiring and valuing old furniture, toys, dishes and books. I treasure those that have been my inheritance over the years. On the other hand, I am realizing that, as valuable as these items may be, they can never be as meaningful or as treasured as the memories of happenings shared with family members and friends over the years. As we get older we draw strength from our roots.

Many of us find great comfort in our memories and want to share them with our families. But age can also cause some of us to forget things. For these reasons, comfort and preservation, I am putting on paper memories that my dad, on my insistence, recorded on tape in his last few years of life. These are accompanied by some of my own recollections, aided by fact-checking with Mom and other friends. Although I am writing mainly about family members, other non-family readers will find interest in the accounts too, maybe even identifying with the experiences.

My parents, Hazel and Howard Gunter, in my opinion, were genuine entrepreneurs. Their experiences are unique, as is the village of Coe Hill, Ontario, south of Bancroft, off highway #62, on highway #620. There they lived and raised their family, and Mom, now 86 and living in Pembroke, would gladly be there today if only health allowed. I moved from Coe Hill in 1960 to begin my teaching career and make a new life, as did most of my age group. Although the times are few, it is good to get together, whether it is for celebrating the annual Coe Hill Fair in late August, a school reunion, or celebrating the life of a mutual friend. Fanning the embers of memories gives us a warmth to carry with us.

The title "The Show Must Go On" was chosen with a dual relationship. Dad, as one chapter in this book will explain, was known to many outside the Coe Hill circle as "The Show Man". As comforting as it is to look back on the dreams he and Mom had and the interesting past life, we that are still on this earth have the duty, and hopefully the desire, to keep *"the show* moving on".

Murray Crosby in his own monthly newsletter 'The Tattler" recently wrote the following little tribute which I thought was fitting to include here: *I tuned into 900 CHML late one night last week as I was driving home. They sometimes play old comedies like Amos and Andy or Jack Benny. On this particular evening I listened to most of Hopalong Cassidy. My memories shot back to my younger days in Coe Hill. Hazel and Howard would run "The Show" as we called it then. It seems that most the townspeople attended those shows. I really looked forward to that night, and enjoyed those old black and whites immensely. Thank you Hazel and Howard.*

Whether you know the Gunters or not, my hope is that you will enjoy the stories in this book.

Heather Campbell (nee Gunter)

> *To forget one's ancestors is to be a brook without a source, a tree without root.*
> Chinese Proverb

Chapter One

Introducing Charles Howard Gunter

Since the writing of this book was motivated by the stories Dad had passed on to me, let me help you know

Dad and Buster

him better. A snapshot acquaints you only with the outside. When I think of Dad I see him with his tongue resting in his cheek as he concentrates on the task at hand. Often this was something mechanical, a motor, a watch, a light. It didn't matter what, he loved the challenge of making it run.

He enjoyed using his own inventions rather than buying the standard equipment. Apparently he had been like that from boyhood, passing time at such pursuits as the making of pipelines from dandelion stems or damming up a creek to create a fishpond.

Dad never smoked but he would leave the table with a toothpick held firmly between his lips and, when he had worn out that one, he had another one ready. Before Mom did the laundry she always checked his shirt pockets for toothpicks. He carried a supply. Wherever he had had a cup of tea or a can of pop through the day you would find a toothpick there. It was Dad's trademark. When he went to the hunting camp he took a pill bottle full of toothpicks with him. Certainly cheaper than cigarettes!

Speaking of checking shirt pockets, Dad would not wear a shirt without a pocket. He had to have a place for his toothpicks and, in later years, his reading glasses. Mom's seamstress skills came in handy whenever Dad was given a shirt without a pocket as a gift. Mom simply found some suitable material and made a pocket.

Dad never went outside without a hat on. He liked the kind with the brim all the way around. Mom made sure they were washable and Dad wore these from spring to fall, graduating to a heavier one with earflaps for the colder weather. Even to go to the outdoor toilet, Dad wore a hat. If he were called outside in his housecoat, he put on his hat.

Belts on pants were a necessity but Dad hated having to change belts from one pair of pants to another. Solution: a belt for every pair of pants! The pants were laundered or dry-cleaned and Mom put the belt in the loops so that when Dad took them from the hanger they were ready. It seemed ironic that a man who could wait forever for a fish to bite didn't have the patience to hunt for belt loops!

Maybe at the root of it all was the fact that Dad didn't care much about clothes for style, just clothes for comfort. He enjoyed lingering each morning in his pajamas, housecoat and slippers, and I expect if he had been left on his own he might not have dressed until lunchtime.

He also hated arriving early for anything, which meant that most times he arrived late!

He loved television and he loved sports, especially hockey, baseball and golf. Dad had never played much baseball or hockey himself, but he coached several teams, usually softball teams. He knew the rules and the moves.

For some reason he never tried to steer me into sports and I did not share this passion with him. I'm sure it must have been a great comfort to him when Allyn (pronounced Allan) was born in 1947, especially as Allyn grew older. It was evident that he certainly had inherited the sports gene.

Dad knew all the major baseball and hockey teams and each player's statistics. It seemed he watched every televised game and groaned with each poor play and cheered with each success. To observe Dad and Allyn watching a game on T.V., you would think they were on the field or on the ice. I'm sure they were exhausted after each game.

Another of his great loves was music. He had a natural gift, which was both a blessing and a curse. The blessing was that he could play by ear any piece he heard, and could play it on guitar, violin, mouth organ, or piano. The curse was that because of this good ear he never learned to read music notation. While Dad was still very young, his piano teacher gave up on him because he did not try to learn to read the notes. Once he heard the tune he could play it. Why bother to learn to play it from the notes on the page? That didn't interfere much with his be-ing in the church choir. He had a wonderful bass voice and followed the notes up or down as he saw them on the page, in perfect harmony. It did grieve him though that he had never learned to read music and I reaped the results of that. He forbade me to play by ear all the while I was studying piano. He thought it was wonderful that I could play a tune I had never heard. Personally, I think there's a place for both skills.

Dad respected nature and he appreciated animals.

He was very much at home in the woods and loved camping, especially the fishing trips to Algonquin Park. He also looked forward to the deer hunt in November each year. At home he liked to have a dog, a cat and even goldfish.

Hunting Gang of 1969
Front: Bill McCaw Jr., Dad
Back: Zane Landon, Dave Wannamaker, Joe Sexsmith, Buster Landon, Jerry McQuigg

I think there was a little bit of the Tom Sawyer nature in Dad. Not having known him as a child I can only go on what I've been told. I particularly like the tale about the garden onions. It seems that, as a young boy, Dad one day had been warned that he was not to pull any more onions out of the garden. Dad liked green onions. What to do? The next time his mother checked, there he was with his hands firmly clasped behind his back, bent over eating the tops off the onions!

Dad wasn't much for extensive repairs. As long as things worked or were livable, he was content. Sometimes we called him Pa Kettle. But the difference was that Dad could talk to you on any subject. That always amazed me and, now that he is gone, I miss that so much. Maybe all daughters think their Dad is the wisest man they know.

Chapter Two

Things My Dad Told Me About "The Beginning"

Dad lived his entire life from 1910 to 1994 in the

Coe Hill area. He lived through the era of the horse and wagon, the motorcar, the gramophone, the radio and the television. Although he was baptized as Charles Howard Gunter, he was commonly known as Howard. He was the oldest of four children born to Henry and Cora (Wilson) Gunter.

Dad and his sister, Mary, 1912

He had two sisters, Mary(Neil) Whitmore and Marjorie(Hubert) King, known as Madge, and one brother, Roscoe (Doris Fisher).

Sign, in front of Elgin and Phyllis-Landon's house, showing Salem Road

When I asked Dad about the origin of the name Coe Hill, he told me that a Mr. Coe, in 1882, accompanied by Harry Johnson, did some prospecting in Wollaston Township. Iron was discovered in the hill east of what at that time was called Salem. A road sign about one and one half miles out of Coe Hill today still bears the name Salem Road. By following it you come to Salem Pioneer Cemetery.

A company was formed to work the mines. The land on which the ore was found was sold to the company by John Batchelor. A settlement grew which was named Coe's Hill. Four hotels were built and there were at least three grocery stores. How jubilant things must have been!

Thanks to this iron ore requiring transportation, a railway was built into the settlement in 1883. Two trains came into Coe Hill each day. 1884 was the glory time for Coe Hill. Unfortunately, because an excessive amount of sulphur was found in the ore, it couldn't be smelted. There was no process to remove that impurity. The mines operated for only about two years and in 1885 had to be abandoned. In that two years, before the sulphur had been detected, large amounts of ore had been mined and stock piled. Huge, deep holes were left as mute evidence in the fields behind our first house on Station Street. Mercifully, thanks to lumbering, the town survived.

Chapter Three

The Wilsons

Howard and his Grandfather Wilson

Dad's family lived about three miles west of Coe Hill alongside his grandfather, Christopher Wilson, and Dad felt privileged to have been able to get to know him so well. In talking to me a few years before his own death, Dad said, "I think my grandpa was in his late 40's before I got to know him, and I've always admired the way he was able to live off his own farm and always had money in his pocket." Then he corrected himself. "I should say, in his purse, because Grandpa had a big leather wallet chained to his belt and he always carried the wallet in his hip pocket."

"They were homesteaders," Dad went on to explain, "Grandpa Wilson acquired his farm under the old Homestead Act." That meant you were granted 100 acres of land as long as you agreed to improve the land, build a house, dig a well, plow ten acres, fence a specified amount, and actually live there. The land was yours at the end of five years if you had fulfilled the agreement.

There were no roads and you had to carry whatever groceries and supplies you needed through the woods all the way in from Millbridge, a distance of at least 20 miles.

Where Grandpa homesteaded he built a log house

ORIGINAL HENRY GUNTER FARM

and then later added to it by building on a framed part. The old original house is still there. It was later bought by the Dave Bird family and that's how I always referred to it, never fully understanding when I was young that it was actually the

HOUSE OF JACK AND CONNIE INGRAM ON
EXACT SAME SITE AS GUNTER FARMHOUSE

original Wilson Farm. It is on the hill between the Henry Gunter farm (now owned by Jack Ingram) and the William Gunter Farm (Where Aunt Madge King, Dad's widowed sister, now lives).

A young Dave Bird, son of Ken Bird, now lives in the Wilson house. I am told that he has changed the inside so much you would not recognize it as the original log house.

When Grandpa Wilson first started out he worked in the woods for the Gilmour people. Grandpa was a great axeman. He could chop either right-handed or left-handed and was in great demand. Because of this he was able to make enough money to build a big barn and start to farm.

It was the days of oil lamps and lanterns but, from all reports, the Wilsons were very comfortable.

Grandpa had a homemade wagon made of pieces of logs about a foot wide around which he had put iron bands. Apparently he could make these iron bands on a small forge that he had in his shop.

Grandpa Wilson was a tall man, about six feet, who always had a moustache. He went to bed when the sun went down and got up always about five o'clock when the sun came up.

Grandpa, in Dad's memory, had room for six cows but always had only four. Maybe that was all he needed and that certainly would be enough to milk. He also had a team of horses and usually five pigs and twenty-five or thirty hens. He managed to live off that. Lumbering was not done much in the winter at that time.

DAD 'S GRANDFATHER WILSON

He kept a fallow field where he would clean up a little bit of land each winter and spring, and plant turnips there. Before hunting season (nobody paid much attention to the hunting laws then) Grandpa would go back to this spot, usually late in the afternoon, and eventually you would hear the sound of the rifle. Then he'd come and get one of the horses and pull the deer up to the house where he would "dress it out". The family now would have venison for the fall and winter.

After Dad had talked about his grandfather for a while he paused, "Before I go any further, I think I should tell you about my Grandmother, because it's true that behind every good man there is a good woman."

Then he proceeded to tell me that his Grandmother's name had been Alida Waddington, before marriage, and that she was a chubby little person about five feet tall. She undoubtedly had helped his grandpa build the house and probably the big barn while raising five children –

George, Lorne, Stella, Lily, and Cora (Dad's mother). She had long black hair worn in two long braids and she always wore an apron. In the cellar there always seemed to be about a hundred jars of pickles, applesauce, and berries of various kinds on the shelves. The apples came from the orchards at both the back and front of their house.

Grandpa and Grandma Wilson

"Grandmother was a very good cook," Dad said, "I can still remember her warmed-up potatoes with pepper, torn-up bread and onion mixed in." (Incidentally, this author has fond memories of Dad teaching me to warm up potatoes that very same way. I think that's why I like to cook enough potatoes to ensure that there'll be left-overs, in my case – "planned-overs"). In talking to Aunt Mary (Dad's oldest sister) who has since passed away, she too mentioned what a good cook her Grandma Wilson had been and the rows and rows of preserves in the root cellar were something she'd never forget.

Grandma Wilson made her own bread and her own butter. She had a butter press that made the butter into pound prints. This butter, along with some eggs, she would take to the store (Rollins General Store, at the time). She dealt these for things the farm could not grow such as tea, salt, and sugar. Dad was impressed with the fact that if Grandpa and Grandma didn't have money to spend, they just didn't buy anything. Grandpa would not go into debt.

Grandpa Wilson was also known as a diviner. He could take a forked branch of a witch hazel tree and, holding it in both hands, he would walk until the wand pulled down in his hands and became almost impossible to hold. That meant that there was water in that spot. Not only was he consulted by the community people who wanted to dig wells, but he also found several good springs on his own property and on the neighbouring Henry Gunter farm, Dad's father's farm. He told Dad's dad (Henry) where to dig the well but it was right on the path between the two farms and Henry did not want to have to build another gate so he moved about six feet to the south and dug the well. The vein came in from the north (where the well should have been) and the well was never a very good one. (I, too, remember that. The water level was always low and it was difficult to dip a pail full.) Henry should have listened to his father-in-law!

Dad remembered the farm having about 50 cleared acres with a creek that ran the full length of the property. There were two marshes on this creek that helped his Grandpa feed the cattle and horses (with marsh hay) over the winter.

Grandpa grew a big crop of field-corn behind the barn. It ripened much later than the sweet corn. Grandpa always told Dad's family to come over and help themselves when he realized their corn was gone. Field corn is reasonably appetizing if it isn't too old. He purposely let it stay in the field until it was quite ripe and then it was feed for the cattle and pigs. Dad helped Grandpa take the cobs off the stalks and husk the corn and these cobs were fed to the pigs. The husks and the stalks would go to the cattle. Dad laughed as he recalled how the pigs could strip the corn kernels off those cobs and spit the cobs out just as slick as if they had hands! Grandpa kept about five pigs so he would have a couple to butcher and some to sell. He usually kept a female so that there would be little piglets to sell in the spring.

The huge field of turnips also provided cattle feed. Dad helped Grandpa in using a pulver to pulverize the turnips for the cattle. As far as he could remember, his Grandpa never had to buy feed for the cattle, not even in the winter.

Dad's own father, Henry, grew an abundance of potatoes and stored them through the winter in what was called 'the potato pit'. Every spring people would come to their house because they were out of potatoes and out of money. His Dad would give them potatoes and, of course, each one said he would pay later. Dad didn't think any of them ever did, nor does he think his Dad really expected any payment.

Grandpa Henry Gunter

Grandma Cora Gunter
At the farm

Chapter Four

Old-Time Religion

It was a delight for Dad to tell about his Aunt Nan, a sister of his father's, who married Seth Welsh. They eventually moved to the States and she became a minister. One time Dad had to meet her at the train in Belleville. He was to drive her to Coe Hill but during Dad's trip to Belleville rain began falling, followed by freezing temperatures. Even with his trusty Oldsmobile he thought a return trip would be too risky. The road was a sheet of glare ice.

Dad said, "Aunt Nan, we're going to have to stay over in Belleville. We can't get home in this."

She said, "Howard, I want to go to Coe Hill. If you drive I'll pray."

And so they started out. There wasn't another car on the road and the road was truly treacherous. Dad could not explain what kept the car on the road. It had to have been his Aunt Nan's prayers. Finally at Madoc they met the sander. From there on the road was better and they arrived safely in Coe Hill. Dad felt like kissing the ground.

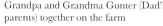

Grandpa and Grandma Gunter (Dad's parents) together on the farm

Aunt Nan was a devout evangelist and always had prayer in the morning. She would come to the barn and say, "Henry, come in and have prayer with us."

His reply was, "Nan, you know I don't have time. If the Lord doesn't know what's good for me, there isn't much sense of me asking Him for it."

He never did go in for prayer, but they did have some good old sing-songs. Dad says his father had a wonderful voice and would have been a great asset to a choir. He sang and played the tambourine and Aunt Nan or Grandma Cora played the organ. They always had a pump organ in their house. In later years there was also Dad's violin and mouth organ.

There were times while Dad's Aunt Nan and Uncle Seth lived at Salem (north of Coe Hill), before they moved to United States, that they would have no food, but they would pray about it and someone would bring them in a bag of potatoes or some eggs or a chicken. In those days unless you had a farm and grew your own crops and animals, there weren't many places to get them. Aunt Nan didn't farm. She and Seth tried to manage on what they made from the store they operated but it didn't always work out. Nonetheless, the Lord did provide, thanks to the generosity of others.

Chapter Five

School Days

Dad started to school when he was seven years old, walking about a mile to the Nugent School, more commonly known as The White School. Here he joined such families as the Wrights, the Millers, the Pettifers and the Blackburns. He well remembered arriving on his first day at school adorned in a corduroy suit and long blond curls that hung to his shoulders. He surmised that he must have been a "pampered little boy" because his mother curled his hair every morning. At school there were three older Gunter girls (probably cousins). Dad remembered them as Connie, Edna and Emma. They took great delight that first day in making fun of Dad, saying, "And what have we here, a girl or a boy?" That night the curls came off!

His mother saved a few and passed them on to Mom who in turn has passed them on to me.

Although Dad was not the one who told me, I have been told by other reliable sources that on the way to school there was a shortcut to take through one of the farms but trespassers had to beware of the farmer's ugly gander. It was wise not to try that shortcut but if you were going to be late for school, it was a temptation. Somehow Dad was always able to convince his sister Mary that she should crawl through

Dad with his curls at 5 or 6 years old

the fence first. If the gander ran at Mary she would scramble back and the two of them took the long route. If Mary did not attract the ire of the gander, Dad followed her. Obviously, even though Dad was the oldest, he was not the bravest.

Dad did train as an airplane mechanic and loved working on engines. His framed certificate showing that he graduated as a Master Mechanic from the Dominion Trade School in Toronto in 1931 now hangs beside his grandson Kevin's Auto Mechanic's Certificate. Unfortunately, at the time Dad graduated, the need for airplane mechanics was minimal and he never did go into that line of work. Nevertheless, tinkering on any type of motor was a lifetime hobby. People even brought their clocks to him for repair. He would work on them in his spare time and, as far as I know, Dad did not charge anything for his labour. He thoroughly enjoyed any type of mechanical challenge.

Dad at his favourite hobby, with Mom either assisting or admiring!

Chapter Six

Married Life Begins

Dad explained that he was a little bit ashamed at age 28 when he got married because all he had was about $100 that he had saved in a cookie jar at the farm. This was in 1938. Mom, (Hazel Soble), at 22, from her pay of $4.00 per week working for Charlie and Nello (Ellen) Rollins, had managed in seven years to save $300. Dad laughed, saying, "I guess I married a rich woman."

Dad and Mom's 'Courting Days'

They were married quietly on June 25th, 1938, at the United Church at Apsley. Dad's only brother, Uncle Roscoe, and a friend, Miss Collins, were their attendants.

Uncle Roscoe, Dad and Mom on Wedding Day

After the ceremony they borrowed Uncle Roscoe's car and drove to the Peterborough area where they stayed in a little cabin. They also visited Aunt Theresa and Uncle George Wilson in Trenton and had a meal there, but it was only a weekend honeymoon. Dad had to get back to his job as the baker in his bakeshop, his chosen occupation at that time. Apparently the car blew a tire just outside Apsley and they almost upset, but secretly I think this was the type of misadventure Dad loved, another chance to use his mechanic's skills. Safely returned to Coe Hill, he was ready to go back to his bake-shop, and Mom worked for a few more months for the Rollins' family.

The following weekend there was a dance, arranged by Mom and Dad's friends, in the town hall. The newlyweds received many gifts, including a large copper clothes boiler filled with a full set of dishes from the Rollins' family.

Dad's first bakeshop was in part of what was called The Company House, owned by the mining company. As soon as possible though, he had a shop built right across from our house on Station Street. Dad was a baker there for about 12 years. Grandpa Soble (Mom's Dad) and Billy Kearns, a friend of Grandpa's, built the bakeshop with most of the lumber being supplied by Grandpa Gunter (Dad's Dad).

Dad's Uncle George Wilson had had a bakery in Trenton, Ontario, and a Lorne Wilder had worked for him. Uncle George had had to fire him because he was too often "under the influence", but he recommended him as an excellent baker and put Dad in touch with him. Dad learned both his bread making and doughnut-making skills from Lorne Wilder. I asked Dad why Grandma didn't teach him to bake and he explained that it's a somewhat different process for bakery bread. You use malt and yeast and of course huge quantities of every-thing. His flour and yeast came in by train.

Dad's bread was so good that for a time the Wes-tons' Bakery truck quit coming into Coe Hill because it wasn't worth the trip. In the beginning Mom helped Dad with wrapping the bread. They used pre-cut wax paper which they wrapped around each loaf and sealed each end by holding it against a large sadiron (the same type as used for ironing clothes) that had been heated in the oven. When Dad and Mom bought the telephone system(see Chapter Seven), Mom was needed full time at home, operating the switchboard and looking after me. I had been born in October of 1940. Pete Doreen, a young lad, was hired to help Dad in the bakeshop.

In time Dad sold the bakeshop to brothers Bert and Don Giles of Coe Hill, passing his skills onto them. At home Dad left the bread and bun-making to Mom. Her buns were a hit not only with the family, but also at church suppers.

Dad now moved from life in the kitchen to life on the road, which you'll read about later in this book.

Cousin Sandra & I with Dad's bakeshop in background

Mom & I (1941) with bakeshop in background

Chapter Seven

Telephone Operations

Wollaston Rural Telephone System had originally been owned and built by Doctor Harding, the village doctor, so he could keep a check on his patients. Charlie Rollins and Norman Gilroy, two town businessmen who definitely contributed to the growth of Coe Hill, purchased it from the doctor. Apparently the switchboard was housed in a little lean-to off the Rollins General Store.

The cost of the purchase was $700 but, when Dad bought it in 1941, he paid only $350, Mr. Rollins' share. Mr. Gilroy simply asked that Dad provide a satisfactory system and that would be payment enough!

There were 25 phones but only 19 of them worked. The six located in the area known as The Ridge were out of order. Because it was wartime, Dad was not able to buy more phones, but he could buy the parts, so he built some phones himself. To me, this was quite amazing, especially when you consider that up until that time Dad had been so afraid of this new technology that he would not even use a telephone!

Mom was already versed in the telephone. She, as a young girl, had helped on weekends to operate the telephone switchboard at Fitzgerald's Store when her family lived in Monteagle Valley. She and Dad made a good team. He understood how it worked and she had the skill and the fearlessness to operate it. She also handled the paper work - the billings, the banking, etc. and had more of a no-nonsense approach than Dad did towards customers who were late with payments.

The troublesome telephone line to the Ridge had pretty much fallen down in Doctor Harding's time. Doctor Harding had put his medical work first and probably did not have time to keep up with line repairs. Dad, using a gas heater, soldered all the joints in the line between Coe Hill and the Ridge. Even after that, poles blew over and trees fell on lines. It wasn't surprising to receive a call from one of the Ridge residents, using a neighbour's phone, to report a malfunctioning phone. Storms definitely played havoc with the early telephone system.

Thunder and lightning made for a pretty scary time in the office part of our house. Sometimes the switchboard provided a real fireworks display with sizzling flashes of green, yellow, and orange flying out of it in all directions. Yes, there was a time or two when I received an electrical jolt while trying to operate during a storm. I wondered why customers risked calling during storms. Reception was always poor, and the operation certainly could be electrifying!

Eventually Dad worked out an arrangement with the hydro in which he could string telephone lines on their poles and this made life easier for everyone. Broken lines and customer-complaints became fewer.

Because it wasn't unusual to have 12 to 16 families all sharing the same line, it made for wonderful eavesdropping on each other's conversations. There was nothing to stop a person picking up the phone and listening to someone else's conversation. I'd imagine it didn't take long to know which ring provided the juicier tales. If you were listening for it, you usually knew by the click that someone had picked up the receiver. I guess this eavesdropping provided "the soaps" of the 1940's and early '50's.

Mom trained three or four people so that they would be able to operate the switchboard when she needed to hire help. Vivian (Walker) Gunter, Verda (Seaborn) McCaw, and our neighbour, Faye(Whitmore) Giles ,were three that I remember who helped out at various times.

I think I was about ten years old when I began helping as an operator, cranking out rings such as four longs and three shorts or six longs and one short. I am sure my arm muscles were better developed than some of my friends who were learning the valuable domestic skills I lack, while I sat at the switchboard. I expect that the people listening for and counting the rings were as tense as I was. It was easy to lose count. What a relief to my arm when the number requested was as simple as one long and two shorts! All lines started out this way when there would only be two or three people sharing, but as the customers multiplied on each line, Dad and Mom had to become more creative in assigning numbers.

Those few families who could afford it had a private line or a two-party line. Most customers, however, were pleased just to have a phone and were content with telephone numbers like 12R6-2 (interpreted: line 12 and you would listen for six long and two short rings). If you were in a hurry to call someone and the line was being used by some neighbour, you simply, politely or not, interrupted them and asked if you could have the line now for your very important call.

Even as a child, I was trusted enough to "mind the switchboard" while my mother took care of domestic du-

Heather Operating the Switchboard About 1956

ties, always within earshot in case I ran into difficulty. As I became older, more and more switchboard time was allotted me. Finally, during school holiday times, I was often left as the sole operator and Grandma was recruited to stay with me while Mom and Dad had a day or so away. I definitely learned more about how telephones work than I did about cooking and sewing. But it was, at that time, a most interesting occupation and one that interested many of my friends too.

No one except former telephone operators could possibly understand what a blessing it was the day that we converted from a cranked switchboard to a button-pushed

Old telephones of the 50's

board. It sure was easier to finger-push six longs than to crank it out. As technology improved, customer phones were converted from crank to dial. I think I was graduating from high school by then. The earliest 'phones were ugly brown wooden boxes hanging on the walls. A black mouthpiece protruded from the middle and a black receiver attached by a cord hung on a hook on the side. You stood in front of the mouthpiece and held the receiver to your ear, replacing it in the holder when finished.

In a later model the receiver and the mouthpiece became one and hung at the side of the phone. Still later, desk sets were introduced to Wollaston Rural customers.

The receiver sat in a hook attached to the set and the whole thing was light enough that you could pick it up and walk around as you talked, as far as the cord would allow. I guess this was the forerunner to our cell phones! Later came the black cradle-phone in which the receiver was cradled in the upper part of the phone just above the dial, much like today's telephones. These cost more and became a bit of a prestige symbol for awhile.

The telephone system played a major part when there was a fire in the village or surrounding area. We would receive a call, usually from a neighbour close to the fire, who would state something like, "Hazel, Clifford Crosby's house is on fire!" Mom would then fly into action, first calling the local fire chief and then alerting everyone who had a telephone by cranking out one extremely long ring on each line, waiting a few seconds for the clicks that signified that various people had picked up their receivers, then announcing where the fire was. She would connect to each line in turn, first alerting those closest to the fire. Fire-fighting for most of those years was voluntary and people wanted to help. Quite often during this scary half hour or so there would be a call coming in to us, and it would be someone who had heard the long ring but had been too late to get the message and they wanted to know where the fire was.

Mom's behind-the-scenes part of helping to fight fires did not go unnoticed. In her collection of keepsakes she has a plaque of appreciation presented to her by The Wollaston Township Fire Department for all her years of dedicated community service.

In the early years of the Wollaston Switchboard, the office, which was really just a part of our dining room, was open only from 8 A.M. until 8 P.M. Can anyone these days imagine not being able to use the phone after 8 P.M.? People who did not have telephones but wished to make a long distance call would come to our house and wait in the dining room while Mom placed the call. The call had to be routed to a Central switchboard at Gilmour, about 20 miles away, and then to a bigger Central at Belleville. Often there would be a delay. When the designated party was reached the customer picked up a phone in the corner of our dining room and had their conversation. When the call was finished, the charge had to be relayed to us from the Gilmour Central and then the customer paid us that amount. What a payphone! What a phone booth!

(And child labour too – Remember, I started as operator number 3 about the age of ten).

The Telephone Office (our house) in 1945 with the roof being raised

How the office looked later

The Central (as our switchboard was called) also performed other favours unheard of today. If your clocked stopped, probably because you forgot to wind it, you simply called us at the switchboard and when you heard our "Number please" you would ask us what the time was. Nowadays, for such a service I'm sure there would be an extra fee. In those days it was part of community-living.

In 1961 when Dad and Mom sold the telephone business they had built it up to 140 phones, about seven times what it had been when they purchased it. Dad had strong political views about monopolies and so he sold to an individual (Charles Collett) rather than The Bell. Unfortunately in a few years time Ma Bell bought it anyway. So much for this fight against monopolies!

Chapter Eight

The Show Man

When Dad sold the bakeshop in 1947, he went "right into the movies"! Dad owned a generator that he carried in his jeep, using it as a source of power to run his movie projector. He had bought this projector from a Harry Taylor who had brought movies to Coe Hill in earlier years. Dad would rent such movies as "Pa Kettle" or "Hopalong Cassidy", or a western starring John Wayne, and during a two-week period would show these not only at the Coe Hill town hall, but also at town halls in Detlor, Fort Stewart, Maynooth, St.Ola, Bancroft, Boulter, Highland Grove, Tory Hill, Wilberforce, and Apsley. He said he could usually take in $100 a night and, even with expenses deducted, that was a lot of money in those days.

The Coe Hill Town Hall (now demomolished) where Dad showed movies

Except for the rare time that Mom or I could go with Dad, he sold the tickets as well as operating the projector.

The admission price was 75 cents for adults and 25 cents for children. People sat on straight-backed wooden chairs and brought their own soft drinks, candy and popcorn. Dad had tried selling these himself for a short while but it proved too much for one person to handle. I have vivid memories of Dad's Bell and Howell Projector and the humming sound it made as its huge reel of movie film wound onto the twin empty reel.

Things didn't always go smoothly. Sometimes during the movie the film would break, often right when suspense was at its highest. The audience would groan in disgust and disappointment. Dad would turn the lights on and patiently rethread the broken end of the film, but that meant that quite a few frames were omitted. Sometimes it meant that the audience had to put their imagination to work, but the show always did go on. Dad would splice the film later at home so it would be intact for the next showing in the next town hall. I've always associated the splicing solution with polish remover because of the strong smell.

Other times the sprocket holes on the sides of the film would get worn or tear completely. The film would then just sit and jump, and the picture on the screen would do the same. The crowd would yell, "Put a ticket in it, Howard!" I was never too sure what Dad did, but he somehow improvised by using a movie ticket to replace the broken sprocket holes so the movie could go on without much of an interruption. I guess it was one of several things that Mom referred to as "cobbled up" but which the family refers to as "a Howard Invention". It was another example of his being able to make mechanical things work and meeting the challenge.

In addition to operating in these makeshift theatres, Dad was also hired by the North Hastings Board of Education to show educational films in about 44 schools. He visited four schools a day, operating on a two-week circuit. At that time no teacher knew how to run a projector, mainly because the country schools did not have electricity. Dad, with his generator aboard his jeep, would visit a school, show the Department of Education films that he had previewed, and provide a few questions for the question-period. Then he would move on to his next school.

Many schools had no way of making the room quite dark enough for movies. As usual, Mom came to the rescue. She used heavy black or navy material, sewed several 36-inch sections together and then put pockets down the sides of these sections. These pockets accommodated 2x2 poles the height of school windows. Dad simply rolled each one end to end and this is how he transported them. He would put these blackout curtains over the windows, start up the generator, and presto – movies! The pupils affectionately called him "the Show Man" and loved to help him set up.

Dad had indelible memories of a couple of schools, one of them being S.S. #7 McClure. Dad had set up in a classroom there during recess one winter day. The bell rang, the children filed in obediently and went to their desks. Dad put the last black-out curtain in place and started the movie. That was the signal! Kapow! Snowballs flew all over that classroom! It seemed each child had carefully concealed a snowball (one wonders just where) and anxiously waited for this opportune time!

This was before the days of electricity and television, which eventually brought the demise of Dad's itinerant "Show Man" job, a job that he had truly enjoyed.

Chapter Nine

From Movies To Insurance

Theatres were becoming dodo birds and so in 1954 Dad and Mom bought a general insurance business from Nick Whitmore of Coe Hill. They simply added another filing cabinet to their makeshift office and operated this business out of their house until 1976. At that time they sold to Gaebel insurance of Bancroft.

From what I remember, Dad did the checking of rates and premium-calculations and Mom did the bookwork and all the filing. In everything they were a team. Dad might remind people that their bill was overdue but Mom was the one to finally cancel them for non-payment. No more free potatoes ! Times had changed.

Customers came to get insurance on a vehicle or building and they also came to report fires, accidents, theft or vandalism. Thank goodness Mom and Dad didn't have to decide on the extent of the claim. That could perhaps have proved a delicate matter sometimes. A claims adjuster was sent by the various insurance companies and, based on his decision, the claim would be paid. I remember one incident where a daughter driving on one of the country roads had collided with a car driven by her father. There were a few red faces but the claim was paid.

As a teenager, I somewhat resented the invasion that this business made into family life. Because the office was part of our house, customers came to pay their bill or do business at any time on any day of the week, apologizing for the hour but still intruding. Mom's advice to me was, "Never operate your own business."

Although I took her advice and became a teacher, there have been times in the harried, hectic teacher-life that I wondered if the home-business idea was such a bad one after all!

Chapter Ten

You Have Mail

Dad said that the two jobs he loved the most in his lifetime were the "show business" and the rural mail route. Dad, under government contract, operated a rural mail route for thirty-eight years, starting mid 1950's.

In fact, there must have been something in the Gunter blood that drew them to working with the Canadian mail. Dad's Uncle, Dick Gunter, was postmaster in Coe Hill from 1929 to 1952. When he and his wife were killed in a car accident, his son Ivan took over. Ivan served in that capacity for thirty-three years, with his wife Irene as assistant for ten years.

When Ivan started in 1952, the Coe Hill Post Office operated out of the front two rooms of their house. In 1978 a new Post Office was built across the road from them. Ivan and Rene continued at their posts until retirement in 1985, at which time Anne Glenn was hired.

Dad sorted the mail in the morning three days a week at the Coe Hill post office. He would leave

The new Post Office built in 1978

Allyn and cousins Judy and Lois Whitmore about 1955 in front of the old Post Office with Lehigh's General Store and Hughson's Service Station in the background

there and deliver on the northern trek to Gilroy, Rose Island and Faraday for one route before lunch, and then to The Ridge as a second route after lunch.

Nothing at home could interfere on mail days with having Dad's lunch ready on the table so that he could keep to his schedule.

Mom made the neatest sorting bags for him out of heavy, sturdy material that rolled easily. I'm not sure where she found that but she took a second layer and stitched deep pockets about six inches wide onto the first layer. Then she labelled each pocket with the name of Dad's customers in the order they lived on his route. Dad sorted the mail into these pockets and then rolled up each bag as bulk allowed. I think he had five or six of these, so as to accommodate all his customers.

Dad And Mr. Bio's Unique Mail Box on R.R. #2

Occasionally he delivered an item from the store too, or ran an errand for a customer, but this was not routine. He tried to not encourage this because he knew the government would frown on it. Absolutely nothing should interfere with the delivery of the 'royal mail'!

Now and then Allyn or Heather or a friend would go with Dad on his route. In later years it was an adventure for the grandkids, Laurie, Kevin, Mark, Steven or Chris, to accompany Dad. Each can attest to the fact that these wooded roads were narrow, crooked, and often full of washboards, but Dad drove as if he were on the freeway. He seemed to have every corner and bump memorized and knew on which section he was apt to meet customer Perry Campbell or a gravel truck. Aunt Carol and cousin Wayne went with Dad once and I don't think they have recovered yet! For 38 years Dad stuck with delivering the mail, sometimes stuck in the mud, stuck in the snow, or stuck in the woods with a flat tire! Nonetheless, he always looked forward to each day of mail-delivery.

Chapter Eleven

Cars of Note

The Plymouth

From as early as I could remember we always drove a used car. It seemed that every two or three years Dad traded the current car, especially if the car had given too much trouble, for one a few years newer. Mom always said that we were just buying someone else's troubles and kept lamenting the fact that we couldn't afford a new one. Dad, on the other hand, enjoyed the challenge of fixing the little problems that occurred.

But finally an 'almost-miracle' happened. Dad brought home the closest thing to a new car that he could afford. It sure looked new. It was a Plymouth station wagon, less than a year old and driven only by the dealer's wife. Huge and heavy, as was their style then, it was a smoked-salmon colour. Mom loved everything about it, from the way it hugged the road to its shiny appearance. Every chance she got she ran it through the car wash. I think Dad was somewhat disappointed to think that his skills probably wouldn't be called upon to baby this car along.

I was about 17, and had been driving for only a year, but I was proud to be allowed to drive this car. One day I drove it the three miles to our cottage and congratulated myself on how well I had done on the narrow, twisting road. When it was time to leave I reminded myself to be careful of the big tree on the driver's side as I slowly backed around to point the car towards home, all the while concentrating on not hitting the front fender. Suddenly I both heard and felt a thump! I got out to check what I really didn't want to see. In my concentration of the front end I had forgotten about the back end and the other trees. Now the back fender bore an imprint of one of those trees. No paint had been damaged, just the shape modified a bit. What to do? Well, at least Mom was away for the day, so it would be Dad who would perform some miracle. And that is just what he did. He surveyed the damage, smiled and shook his head a little and headed for his toolbox. Out came his rubber mallet and underneath the fender he went. Occasionally he surfaced to check his work and then disappeared again to give another tap or two. When he was done it would have taken a trained eye to know that there had been a mishap. Dad never said a word to Mom about it nor did I until just yesterday, some forty years later. She says that she certainly remembers the car but not the incident. Even as we talked and I told her all the details, I knew that if Dad could be here he'd be adding, "There was no sense worrying about it. They're making cars every day you know."

The Nash

One more early car experience comes to mind. In 1956 Dad and Mom owned the Nash. It was green and white and big and heavy and had a wide bench-like projection from the trunk area to the back bumper. It practically invited people to sit down on it. That is just what some of my Vacation Bible Students did as I pulled away from the church, heading to our house at the far end of the village. I was aware that they were there but I was going very slowly, and these were young teenagers who I felt could take care of themselves.

As fate would have it, a policeman just happened to be in town that day and he did not share my view. The first thing I knew the cruiser was behind me flashing its headlights and spinning its cherry! Of course the kids all jumped off and scattered and I was left to do the explaining. The conversation was pretty tense until he learned that I was Howard Gunter's daughter. Whew! I was inexplicably let off with only a reprimand. Maybe he owed Dad a favour. The whole incident sticks vividly in my mind even today and I can honestly say that I've had personal experience with the expression "I thought I'd wet my pants".

Car On The Loose

Dad was a very wise man, in my opinion, but the wisest can still err in judgment. When my brother Allyn was just a toddler, Dad used to take him in the car when he had errands to do or quick visits to make. For some reason, probably because he was in a hurry, he seldom took him into the store or house he visited. But he did usually turn off the car engine. That is except for a very cold winter day when he visited Grandma at the farm on the hill. He was just dropping off a bottle of medicine so he knew he would not be long. Rolling the window down a bit, he left the car running , mainly because this Austin had a habit of not starting in the cold. To keep it running he had pulled the choke out a little, but pulled the emergency on. The choke being out caused the car to vibrate intensely. I guess the vibrations kept gaining momentum until the emergency brake would not hold back the horsepower!

Dad came out of the farmhouse door in time to see the little Austin careening slowly down the hill. He ran, heart in mouth, wondering how this trip would end. He could have used some of his Aunt Nan's prayers about then. But she or some other angel must have been watching overhead. Just like it was planned, the car swerved toward the overgrown lilac bushes before it had picked up too much speed and came to rest there, motor still running. Allyn's terrified screaming was apparently as loud as the motor. He had not enjoyed this thrill ride. The good news was that he was not hurt and, by some miracle, no damage had been done to the car. Dad was forever grateful for the 'flower-power' that saved the day.

Safe At Home
Heather with baby-brother Allyn on
the porch step of Station St. house

Chapter Twelve

Fisherman Tales

Dad's Fishpond Story

At 86 years of age, Dad told me this story as if it had just happened yesterday.

With his family living so close to Snow Lake, it seemed Dad had always been interested in fish. When he was about 10 years old he built himself a fishpond. He said if he had been a boy today he probably would have had an aquarium, but in those days that wasn't possible. He used a shovel and dug a big trench about eight feet by six feet. Grandpa had a spring that formed a small pond and Dad then drained water from that into his trench and made his own little pond. Then he went down to the lake and caught some small fish, mostly sunfish and bass. He put these into his new fishpond and tended it the same as anyone would an aquarium. Each day he took the fish some breadcrumbs or some rolled oats. He became quite attached to these fish. They were colourful and thriving and very much at home in their new surroundings. Some water plants had grown there which afforded them some protection. Dad was pleased with his "family".

This daily feeding ritual continued until early one summer morning when, on the way down to the pond to see his fish, he startled a big blue heron that had not been expecting him. The heron took off when he saw Dad but the damage had already been done. There wasn't a fish left.

Dad sounded sad recounting the tale even after all these years. "That was the end of my fish pond," he said. "I didn't ever restock it."

Painful as it was, Dad had learned first hand about Mother Nature's food chain.

Never Go Hungry

Dad, clearly happy, with his catch of the day!

Fishing was one of Dad's passions. He loved the tranquility of nature. He loved the sport. And he loved food! Eating outdoors made it taste even better. Grandson Mark remembers his first fishing trip to Anstruther Lake with his Dad and Grandpa Howard, not so much for the fishing element, but more because that was the first time he had eaten fried Spam and instant potatoes!

Dad never asked Mom to pack meals for his trips to Algonquin Park. He took the required number of days' food with him and cooked it there. He never skimped on quantity. These trips always involved a portage, toting both the canoe or boat and the food. My husband Frank, who went with Dad a few times, can attest to the hard work involved on these portages. He chuckles about Dad's resolve that whatever food they took in to the lake they had to eat so as not to have to carry it out. His most vivid recollection of the earnestness of this resolve is seeing Dad, on the last day of the trip to Burnt Island Lake, sitting on a log eating a whole can of peas before they set off on the homeward portage!

Angels Watching Over

Dad and Uncle Bill Soble enjoying being winched out of the water after a fishing trip

Sometimes the waters would get a little rough while they were out fishing. Frank remembers a time that this happened and they resolved that they'd better head for shore. The little fiberglass boat battled its way through the waves as they increased in intensity. Dad kept his eye fixed on shore and his hand on the throttle. Frank hung on, dodging the spray. Just as they reached shore the whole end of the bow broke out of the boat and the water gushed in. Frank and Dad pulled the boat up on shore, surveying the damage.

"Boy, I'm glad that didn't happen any sooner," Dad said. "You know I can't swim a stroke!"

That revelation and the realization of his responsibility certainly unnerved Frank a bit. Imagine a man who spent as much time on the water as Dad did, not being able to swim!

What did they do?

Well, although there was not a soul in sight, some-

Proud Fishing Buddies
Dave Wannamaker and Dad display their catch!

one had left a boat on shore near by. It was in good shape so they "borrowed" it, went down to the store at the marina, bought a patching kit, brought it back, returned "the loaner" to its spot and got on with patching the boat.

Did they catch fish on these trips? Yes, indeed. They brought home the best trout ever, to be expertly cooked by Mom and shared with the rest of us.

One More Fishing Story

A recent visit with Doug Wilson in Oshawa, a first cousin to Dad, resulted in an evening of reminiscing.

Uncle Lorne Wilson, his son Doug, Dad with his guitar and sister Marjorie

Doug's most vivid memories of Dad center around fishing. His Dad, Lorne, and my dad, Howard, spent many summer weekends in a fishing boat. Doug said he felt cold just telling about the weekend that he, as a young man, went with the two dads to Burnt Island in Opeongo Lake, Algonquin Park.

At dusk on a cool, damp evening they put up their tent. Even before they had finished setting up, the rain started. It rained in torrents. The tent leaked and the water ran through the tent, underneath his air mattress at one end and out the other. Doug had all his clothes on, trying to keep warm, but soon they were all soaked from the top layer of clothing to the skin. He said that he could never remember being so wet or so cold!

By dawn he and Uncle Lorne sat hugging themselves, their teeth chattering, lamenting about how they were freezing. Dad, seemingly undisturbed by the weather, found some reasonably dry wood and built them a fire. With great relief they were huddled around it, enjoying the warmth and drying out a bit, when a park ranger paid them a visit. He was there to notify them that fire-building in the park was prohibited! Recalling this, Doug laughed, saying, "Now one would wonder, on an island with water all around, how much damage a fire could do, especially with everything so rain-soaked!"

To make this an even more memorable morning, the catch of lake trout from the evening before which they had left strung on a fishing line and hanging in a tree, was now just a string of fish heads! The bulk of their catch rested in the tummy of some four-footed woodland visitor! Well, at least they still had the heads as proof if anybody questioned this particular fishing story.

Knowing Dad, I'm sure they cooked a good breakfast of bacon and eggs on their camp stove, and got into that boat, baited their lines and started over. I can't recall Dad ever coming home from the Park without a good catch. It was always made even better by Mom's special coating of an egg, milk, and crumb mixture on each piece before she fried it in butter. Delicious! Maybe even worth freezing for!

Chapter Thirteen

Pets and Unpets

Cats Do Have Nine Lives

My parents told me that they had had a lovely cat during the first two years of their marriage, right up to the time that they brought me home from the hospital as their first-born precious bundle. It seems that the cat took one look, meowed to be let out and never came back! Talk about a nose out of joint!

But, as we all know, there's never a problem finding another cat. From as far back as I can remember we always had a cat in the house.

Dad was a great fisherman, but usually brought the fish home to be cleaned. Somehow on one occasion, our cat, who was perhaps a year or so old, was allowed to sample the parts meant for the garbage. In the one fish head there still was the dreaded fishhook. I guess Dad either had missed seeing it or had not been able to twist it out. It was soon apparent that the poor cat had this hook caught in the side of her neck. It was useless to try and retrieve it. She wouldn't be still and, even if she had, none of us felt we had the surgery skills to cut out a fishhook.

We might have considered driving the long hour and a half trek to the nearest veterinarian except that it was the weekend and offices were closed. Dad loved animals and maybe he felt responsible for the cat's plight. Without much discussion he lovingly loaded the poor creature into the car and drove to our family doctor in

Bancroft, about a thirty-minute drive. The office being closed, Dad rang the emergency bell and explained the problem. The doctor ushered him in through the back door and prepared the anaesthetic, wanting to get this whole thing over with before he would be discovered operating on a cat! (Probably today there would be some law that would make this a violation!) Well, the fishhook was removed all right and the wound stitched up, but the doctor was aghast at how difficult it was to anaesthetize this cat. He said that it took as much anaesthetic as he would have used for nine people. The cat suffered no long-term effect and was the much-loved pet for many more years. Fish heads were no longer on the menu!

Why Am I So Tired?

Then there was the more recent cat that I gave to my parents as a kitten when Dad was sick and Mom was his nurse. It was a stressful time for everyone and I thought a kitten would add some levity to things. I guess it did all right! It loved to play, especially after Dad and Mom had gone to bed. Mom felt that the kitten was the reason that she was not getting her rest, so one night not only did Dad get a sleeping pill but so did the kitten. (Where are the animal rights people when you need them?) The kitten did try to get up the next morning, but after a staggering trip to its bowl, it careened its way back to its spot at the end of the couch and stayed there all that day, that night, and most of the next day! I'm happy to report that it did return to normal and today is a beautiful cat, much adored by Mom's great granddaughters, Amanda and Jessica.

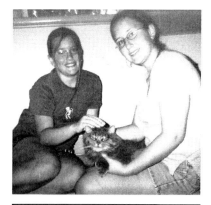

Great Granddaughters, Jessica and
Amanda Gervais, and their beloved cat
Pepper

Rainbarrel Rescue

My mother had had another cat episode when she
was still a child at home. She was the oldest child and the
only girl at that time and had been allowed to have a
beautiful Persian cat for a pet. She named it Fluffy and it
was always near her.

Grandma Soble baked bread every Saturday in the
big wood stove in the kitchen. A fire was first made to heat
the oven. Grandma, as usual, slammed the oven door shut
to heat the oven as fast as possible while she and Mom
were doing other chores in the kitchen. In time they heard
what sounded like the faint mewing of a cat. Where was it
coming from? It seemed to be the oven. Mom opened the
oven door cautiously, peeked in and then started screaming. There, inside the oven, was her beloved Fluffy, looking quite lifeless. Occasionally Fluffy had curled up on the
open oven door, but this time I guess she had crawled in
further and Grandma had not noticed her.

Mom's screaming brought Grandpa from his back-yard blacksmith shop. He sized up the situation in a hurry, scooped Fluffy up and, with Mom still screaming hysterically, Grandpa ran outside to the rain barrel at the corner of the house. He doused Fluffy up and down in the cold water a few times until she yowled almost as loud as Mom and began clawing to free herself.

Grandpa was certainly Mom's hero that day and, once again, the old adage of a cat having nine lives had been proven.

Dog Days

Mom didn't much care for dogs, especially in the house. Dad, on the other hand, loved dogs. He always kept a dog for hunting purposes, so he said, but the dog was kept outside on a chain tied to the clothesline near its doghouse. I particularly remember Chief, a brown, white and black mixed breed, but predominantly hound. Chief

had a habit of getting free from the chain. I was never sure how he managed it, but I sometimes suspected that my father had a hand in it. Anyone who loves dogs knows that they need exercise. Chief seemed to be well-known in the village, and had learned to fear a broom. We surmised why one day when friend Muriel who lives at the other end of the village asked Dad how Chief had enjoyed the roast. Apparently Muriel

Dad with Grandson Mark and his pet, Simon

was in the habit of using her woodshed as a summer kitchen and had set the roast on a table until she could clear a place for it in her fridge. She came on the scene just in time to see Chief leaving with the roast!

Incidentally, Chief's death a few years later was due to poisoning. I guess even though he was well-known in the village, he wasn't necessarily well-loved!

Dogcatcher Daze

A few years before the saga of Chief, Dad had been appointed dogcatcher for the village. I was never sure whether he had volunteered or been commandeered. Some relatives did a lot of teasing about this assignment. I really don't know why. Perhaps they thought it an embarrassment.

One night not too long after this appointment, we were awakened by what sounded like a dog's howling. It seemed to be right under Mom and Dad's bedroom window. Mom raised the window to have a look below. There was howling for sure, but not from a dog. Chained to a tree was a very drunk villager who was being egged on by one of our mischievous but also very drunk relatives! Mom, of course, recognized them and they both suffered the wrath of her tongue, which could be more of a deterrent than any broom! The next day, to their credit, this pair made a contrite and sincere apology. All was forgiven and Mom could eventually laugh about it all. Very shortly after that episode Dad resigned as dogcatcher.

Jughead

Many things besides wood were stored in the wood-shed attached to the back of our house. One of these things was the garbage, waiting for Dad's weekly trip to the garbage dump. Of course the outside door to the woodshed was seldom shut. People came and went from our kitchen via the woodshed.

The smell of a skunk was not an uncommon thing in the village on any summer evening. One night though, we noticed the smell seemed particularly strong in our kitchen. Upon opening the door to the woodshed we soon knew why. Mom had thrown an unwashed jar into the garbage. That jar had contained some kind of meat and I guess the smell enticed one of thc village skunks. There, thrashing around in our woodshed, was a skunk with its head ensconced in the jar. Try as it might, it could not pull itself free and it was becoming quite frantic and the shed quite perfumed by the defence-mechanism that all of us wanted to avoid. In those days there was no Ministry of Environment office to call nor any Animal Control officer (the dog catcher did not handle such things). We had no choice but to let nature take its course that evening and we exited by the front door if leaving the house.

That skunk did eventually make its way out of the shed, but not out of the jar. My father kept an eye on it and, rather than have it in misery, he waited until it was in the field behind our house and, from our clothesline step he trained his rifle on it and ended its predicament. I guess he buried it, although none of us chose to attend

Jughead's burial. We all were a little more careful about garbage storage after that, but it was a long time before our visitor's perfume faded away in that woodshed.

Chapter Fourteen

Stories About Mom Before Dad was a Part of Her Life

The House Fire

Mom in 1930 standing in front of the Soble House in Coe Hill.

Mom did not come to Coe Hill until she was close to 13 years old. Grandpa and Grandma Soble and family moved to Coe Hill around 1929 and lived in the house later occupied by Jim Ungers and still later by the Tinneys.

Mom's childhood was spent in Maple leaf and Monteagle. She only recently told me about this happening, which dates back to about 1919 when they lived in Maple Leaf.

Mom and her brother Bill were the only children at that time in what later would be a family of nine. It was maple syrup-making season. Grandma Soble was boiling down sap in the summer kitchen, a room connected to the main house but used only in the summer. This room had a cook stove and some basic pieces of furniture all supported by a one-ply wooden floor.

On this particular day Grandma stoked up the wood fire, checked the sap which was far from the boiling point and then decided to take the two youngsters and go and see if her neighbour needed any help. She bundled up Uncle Bill in his blanket, took my mother Hazel by the hand, and they walked briskly to the neighbours on the next farm. The teakettle was always ready for visitors and Grandma was enjoying a cup of tea. When the neighbour got up to refill their cups she gasped as she looked out the window, "Maria, your house is on fire."

By the time a bucket brigade was formed, the house was beyond saving. All that could be done was to prevent the fire from spreading. The family stayed with the neighbours that night. The next day they surveyed the pile of gray ashes. Nothing from the house had been saved. Mom said that as they kicked through the ashes the only thing she can remember that they found was her little tin baby cup. It was cleaned up and kept as a memory of their life at Maple Leaf, but the family moved to a new farm at Monteagle and started over. Mom does not remember any blame being laid. It was thought that probably some hot coals had jumped out of the stove when Grandma had stoked the fire and they had smoldered on the dry wooden floor, finally igniting, and quickly became

Although not the house in the above story, this picture is the Coe Hill house in which Mom's parents, Richard and Maria Soble, lived in 1930. In 1980 when it burned, it was owned by Richard Tinney.

Mom & sister Janet, Ameliasburg

an uncontrollable inferno.

I can only imagine the heartache such a tragedy must have caused. Grandma and Grandpa never talked to me about it. Perhaps it was best forgotten as they got on with their lives and family.

Grandpa was a blacksmith and practised this trade while in Coe Hill, but later moved to Ameliasburg to set up a shop there.

What People Don't Know Won't Hurt Them

Mom worked as hired help for the Rollins Family who owned the local grocery store and the Shell Oil Dealership. Sometimes she had duties in their home, and other times she was needed in the store. Some of her memories are still pretty vivid.

In order to iron most things in those 1930's, you had to sprinkle them with water, roll them up in a towel, letting them sit until they were uniformly dampened, and then iron them quickly before they dried out. It was a real art to iron a man's long-sleeved white shirt so that it had no wrinkles. It had to be just the right degree of dampness and it was best to leave the sleeves until last or they would simply become wrinkled again as you flopped the shirt around doing the other sections. Imagine Mom's despair when after she had painstakingly dampened, rolled , laboriously ironed and hung the shirt on its hanger, she was told it wasn't acceptable and watched as it was grabbed and rolled into a ball and she had to start over. We should be so thankful today for dryers and permapress materials.

But there were humorous happenings too. Once Mom was hurrying to put the platter of chicken on the table before the company came to the table. As she misjudged the distance in reaching over the highback dining room chairs, the whole platter did an upside down dive to the floor. Mom froze in horror but she was quickly advised, "Never mind Dearie, just scoop it all back onto the platter, wipe the floor up well and no one will be the wiser." And no one was!

Then there was the time that a good customer brought to the store some of the butter she had made . Many people in those days churned the cream from the milk of their cows into butter. The trade and barter system was alive and well then too so it was quite common for people to exchange eggs from their farm for a pound of tea at the store, or potatoes for cheese. This particular lady, however, wanted to exchange butter for butter! Why? Because a mouse had got into it and even though she had cut that part off and what was left was perfectly clean-looking, she just couldn't eat it. But she reasoned that no one else would know the difference. Mr. Rollins agreed with her, took her butter to the basement, put it in the press used for the commercial butter, wrapped it in the commercial wrapper and handed her back what was really her own butter, saying, "What people don't know won't hurt them." She went cheerfully on her way and remained a good customer.

Maybe only humorous in hindsight, but certainly not at the time, were Mom's 4:00 A.M. risings on the mornings that Mr.Rollins Junior was going fishing. No, she didn't go with him. She was up at that hour to make his lunch that consisted of boiled eggs and bread and butter. Maybe the Rollins family was secretly training Mom to be the good, biblical wife mentioned in Proverbs 31:15 who 'riseth while it is yet night, and giveth meat to her household'!

Although she would have preferred to have made this lunch the night before, when you were the hired help and did not have the strength of today's unions behind you, you did as you were told. Mom was earning $4.00 per week, which in the '30's was standard pay.

In spite of what may sound like militant expectations as far as Mom's work duties, the Rollins family was always very appreciative of Mom. Even after she had left their employment to become a full-time wife, they always remembered her on special occasions, especially Christmas. After I was born I too received an annual Christmas gift from them. One gift - treasured by me then and still today - was a child's tea set in the "blue willow" pattern. When granddaughters Jessica and Amanda were much younger we had some tea parties using this very set of dishes. Ironically, I was always the maid who did the serving at these parties!

Chapter Fifteen

Early Snowmobiling

Dad loved snowmobiling. He enjoyed tinkering with the engines and the follow-up testing them out on the trails. In the earliest years of this sport I remember few regulations. We

Dad in 1972 driving the Rupp with Kevin and Laurie on the sleigh

made our own trails and enjoyed a few hours in the fresh air. As the sport became more popular Dad became quite involved in helping to create and maintain regulated trails. These were mapped out and linked with other areas. Licensing of machines and council-budgeting for trail maintenance became part of life.

Grandkids Kevin, Mark and Laurie on the sleigh behind Grandpa's Skidoo

A day from early snowmobiling times is forever locked in my mind. Our daughter Laurie was about three years old. Dad, my husband Frank, and myself had all been snowmobiling and had just returned to the backyard. We left Laurie sitting on the one machine as we adults hopped off to discuss the sights of the trail we had just covered. Suddenly we realized that Laurie and machine were taking off and no amount of screaming, "Let go, let go," convinced her to do so. In fact, the machine started going faster and faster as it careened around the yard. As she became more frightened she hung on to the handlebars tighter and tighter, which meant that she was squeezing the throttle harder. Remember, this was in the early days of snowmobiling. Neither the Bolen D'iable Rouge nor Husky's top speed would have been more than thirty miles an hour but, thank goodness, our novice never reached this speed.

Dad, in his quick thinking, ran fast enough to be able to jump on the machine with Laurie as she careened by for the second circle, and he quickly hugged her to him and released her grip while applying the brake. What could have been a disaster ended happily. We were able to laugh about the D'iable Rouge living up to its name (Red Devil), but three adults had certainly learned a lesson about turning off their machines before leaving them unattended. Laurie, now in her thirties, says she occasionally still relives the event as a nightmare.

Talking about the early snowmobiling days brings back other memories of a not-so-busy lifestyle. Frank and I enjoyed packing wieners, buns, tea, and even marshmallows. We'd stop, usually near a lake, find some of the brush left behind by those who had helped to clear a trail, build a fire and cook our hot dogs. A lunch made over an open fire tastes so good. I can't remember us worrying about getting back to keep appointments like we tend to do now, some thirty years later. Television had not yet made addicts of us, and we either took the kids with us or left them with Grandpa and Grandma. Life was good. Life was simple.

Frank with Laurie on the Rupp in 1973

Allyn and his son, Christopher,
ready for a ride in 1984.

Chapter Sixteen

Childhood and Teen Days
Grandma's Pantry

The heavy wooden door to this room was always kept shut. The door was at the corner of the kitchen but so hidden by a rack of coats that one could easily miss it. I can't remember how old I was when I was first allowed in but I'll never forget the delectable smells that filled this pantry of Grandma Gunter's, Dad's mother (Cora). The overall aroma was one of sweetness, probably emanating from the vanilla used in all Grandma's baking. There was absolutely no heat in this room, so it was a wonderful place to be sent in the summer, but in the winter the trips in and out were made very quickly.

Huge cotton bags of flour and sugar sat on the floor in one corner. Cupboards lined three walls and the one cupboard had a projecting metal counter. On this counter there always sat a big tin full of Grandma's sugar cookies. They were a perfect shade of brown, sprinkled with white sugar and crowned with fat raisins. Sometimes on the bottom of the cookie would be a little bit of white flour. I accepted this without question and it was years later in my own kitchen I realized that Grandma must have always dusted her cookie pans with flour. I had simply been buttering mine and often ended up with cookies whose bottoms were scorched.

This room was the home for Grandma's Christmas

Grandma and her visitors: Anne Giles, Wilma McCaw, Kay Giles, myself, Lois Whitmore, Sandra Whitmore. (About 1950)

cake, her famous Christmas plum pudding and thick white sauce, her date squares and her bread puddings. Behind those cupboard doors rested her secret ingredients, but I cannot remember having the pleasure of opening any of these doors. Nor did I ever seem to be on the spot when Grandma did her baking. Grandma's secrets could never be spilled by me. Now, how I wish I had been just a little more inquisitive.

Laundry Mondays

A recent shortage of water and our efforts at recycling took me back to "wash days" when I was a child. Water was precious. We had a choice of carrying drinking water (hard water) in pails from a well we shared with our neighbours, the Tivy family, or we could use from our cistern of soft water. The soft water required less soap and supposedly produced a better wash and cleaner, softer clothes. An eaves trough ran around the entire roof of our house and a pipe ran vertically from that to the cistern.

The cistern was a cement-lined shaft in the ground covered over with a heavy board which we had been warned not to go near for fear of falling in. The water level in it depended on how much rain we received. In an extremely dry year you could have your cistern filled with water from a tanker-business. I think that water came from a nearby lake. Eventually we had a hand pump in the kitchen to pump from this cistern. In the beginning it had been a pail on a rope.

Washday began early in the morning with the filling of a huge copper boiler with water that was put on the wood stove to heat. With all this effort, it was important to use that water as many times as possible.

The first machine of which I have much recollection was a white pot-bellied one with a wringer on top. The machine was three-quarters filled with hot water, soap was added along with the dirty white clothes, and you pushed a bottom handle to the right and the agitator in the center of the machine started. The tea towels and dishcloths and sheets were washed first in very hot water. When they were deemed clean you grabbed a corner of each and gently guided it to the rollers in the wringer. If you didn't pull your fingers back in time, you risked having a hand or your entire arm drawn into the wringer before you could get the pressure released.

With soap and water squeezed out, each item now dropped into a huge washtub of clean rinse water. You swished them around in this water, swung the wringer over this tub and started the now-rinsed clothes through the wringer again and into a clothesbasket. I guess this is how we got the saying "she/he's been through the wringer".

The wicker clothesbasket was then lugged outside to the clothesline step. Each item in the basket was pinned with clothespins to a clothesline and you hoped for a good breeze to dry the clothes.

Another load of "whites" was put into that same

wash water and the whole process repeated again. When all the white clothes had been laundered, then you began washing the coloured, beginning with the least-soiled and working up to the real "grubbies". I think we changed the rinse water but not the wash water.

When the entire wash was done, a pail was set under the machine, a spigot was twisted and the water drained and was carted, one pailful after another, outside. Sometimes it was used to water gardens if it was an extremely dry year. Quite often the floor was mopped with the rinse water, using a mop made from rags.

There was usually a little bit of handwashing in a small tub or sink. This was for delicates or for clothes that had a bad stain and needed pre-treatment. For these latter items, you stood a glass washboard in the tub and used a bar of soap and lots of friction as you rubbed the spot against the ridges of the washboard. Then into the big machine the garment went.

All this was to be accomplished on a Monday. Once the clothes were dry, they were collected from the line, folded and put into a basket and on Tuesday the ironing of these clothes could begin! Were these really the good old days?

As with any task though, the way to make it easier is to have some company and good conversation as you work. That eventually happened to the Monday washday at our place, for a few years anyway. A minister, Reverend Frank Whitely and his wife, Helen, arrived in Coe Hill with an electric washing machine. Coe Hill had no electricity. But because of Dad having a traveling movie-business, we had a generator. The end result was that Reverend Whiteley's machine was moved to our house where we supplied the power, and Mom and Mrs. Whitely did their laundry together. I guess this was the forerunner to the "laundromat"! Reverend Whitely was supposed to stay at home and baby sit, but hardly a Monday went by that he didn't make the trip across the road, baby in-tow, always before the washing was finished because he enjoyed the laughter and chit-chat so much.

It proves that anything in life, even doing the laundry, is more fun when you share it with someone else.

Making Butter the 50's Style

Well, it wasn't really butter. It was margarine. To save money many families, including ours, were using it. The trouble was, you bought it as a white mass in plastic bags pretty much the same size and quality of our present litre milk bags. It had much the same appearance as shortening does today. Inside this plastic bag, in the very centre of the white mass, was a round capsule of deep orange food colouring. In order to pass this pale product off as "butter", it required a person to break this capsule by pressing hard on the bag and then to start squeezing the bag until the colour was a uniform light yellow throughout. That took a lot of squeezing. Mom usually assigned the job to me and my hands ached when I was done. The bag was then put in the refrigerator so that the contents became firm enough to slice and be served as butter to those that didn't know any better. I was certainly glad when the government gave permission for the sale of pre-mixed, coloured margarine and my job of "making butter" became obsolete!

Taffy Making

One favourite memory I have of our church Young People's group when I was in my early teens, is the wonderful spring taffy-pulling parties we had. I guess we were badly spoiled because we did not have to go to the bush,

Front: Nello Foran, Gail Graham, Jean Marshal, Heather Gunter, Sandra Whitmore, Wilma McCaw
Back: Betty Holland, Heather Graham, Mrs. Hancock (leader), Bernice Vader, Faye Marshal, Marjorie Tivy

or even step outdoors, for that matter. The maple syrup was heated by our leaders on the stove in the church kitchen. When it reached a certain temperature, large metal pans full of crisp white snow were brought into the Sunday School hall at just the opportune moment. We poured the hot syrup over the snow and watched as it stiffened into warm, sticky treacle. Then the real fun part began. We pulled the sticky treat off the snow and kept pulling and twisting it, folding it in half and pulling and twisting and repeating this over and over until we had a tasty length of blonde-coloured taffy. Some of us just ate it direct from the snow without doing the pulling. My mouth waters at the memory. I hope that Mr.Gilroy, a stalwart of our church who was the wonderful provider of this abundance, has a special star in his crown and somehow knows that the memory of this pleasure lives on.

The Case of the Prize Flowers

When I was about 12 years old I was encouraged to try for a prize in the Coe Hill Fair by planting and growing some flower seeds. Following the package directions I planted marigolds and zinnias in the flowerbed underneath our dining room window. Thanks to the sun blessing them each morning and my faithful watering, they grew really well. I was proud of them.

Apparently my brother Allyn, seven years younger than I, didn't fully understand about the flowers and the fair. He was outside playing with his friend Betty Wannamaker from next door, who was about four years old at the time. At noon I was sent to get Allyn for lunch. I stepped outside the front door to call him but ended up screaming his name and a few other things as well! There in little piles lay my prized flowers, each one snapped off just below the blossom. Any dreams I had of winning a money-prize for them at the fair had just become a nightmare. Of course my screams brought both my mother

Allyn and neighbour, Betty Wannamaker, about 1950

and Betty's mother running. I was sobbing out my sad story of how I had nothing to show at the fair. Allyn and Betty were sobbing because they now knew what they had done was wrong, although they didn't really understand why. They had been helping they said. Finally everyone had calmed down enough to hear Betty's Mom, Madge, saying, "Heather, don't worry about the fair. I'm really sorry for what the kids have done and you can take some of my flowers and show them." So that is what I did, and I won first prize! The fact that I had won a prize on flowers that weren't mine did not really bother me at the time. I guess I felt the case had been settled satisfactorily out of court!

Early High-Tech

For many years the privilege of listening to the radio required the purchase of a licence. I still remember one time when the policeman, Stan Palmateer, was standing inside our front door while Mom, balancing on a wooden chair, was frantically searching the top shelf of the kitchen cupboard, all the while declaring that she was sure she had renewed that radio licence. When she couldn't produce it, the patient Constable said, "Mrs. Gunter, my files show you have not renewed and I'm sorry, but you will have to pay the fine." Mom can't remember now whether the fine was $6.00 or whether that was the cost of the licence, but she had to pay both, at that time a hefty sum. Mom was days recovering from that "crime and punishment" experience. Sometimes there's just no way to escape the arm of the law!

Always Indebted to Simpsons

When you live in the country, an hour or more from any big city, it's difficult to take advantage of the sales, especially in the winter when weather and roads are so unpredictable. I really wanted a new winter coat, had saved the money I made delivering papers, and had picked out the coat I wanted in the big winter catalogue sent to everyone by the Simpsons Company (later part of Simpsons-Sears). The coat was red with double-breasted big white buttons and had a fabric belt trim at the back with one white button in the middle. Since what I had saved was not equal to the price quoted (I believe it was $49.99), Mom had said to wait until the winter sale catalogue came out and it would probably be reduced. I waited patiently, imagining myself elegantly attired in this coat.

Alas, when the sale catalogue did arrive, there were pages and pages of coats on sale, but not the red one that

I had so counted on. I was heartbroken and asked if maybe we couldn't go to Belleville or Peterborough to shop. That seemed to be out of the question, but Mom did write a letter to Simpsons explaining her teenage daughter's financial circumstances and how far from personal shopping we were and how I had dreamed of owning this coat. She suggested that they consider sending it to me at half price. In about a week a large parcel arrived C.O.D. for $25.00. My hands shook as I opened it. Inside was my coveted red coat. I wish now that I had taken the time to write to the kind soul who at that time answered the mail at Simpsons and handled odd requests such as my mother's. Surely he or she must have been from a small town and understood what rural life is like. Credit goes to my mother too, for her undaunted spirit in making such a request.

Here I am standing beside Frank and wearing that much beloved red coat from Simpsons

Wheel Love

It was a black 1941 Chevrolet in the year of '57. Frank, my 18-year-old high school sweetheart, was the proud owner. Although I was not his first girlfriend, this was the first car he had ever owned. To me, at 17 years of age, the car was wonderful and 'the driver' was perfect in every way. I was absolutely in awe of how he could use the foil from a cigarette package to make the headlights function after a fuse had blown. The most romantic aspect of this car was that it had a large hole in the floorboards on the passenger side which meant that I had to sit very close to 'the driver' so as not to get covered with dust or water puddles (depending on the weather). We often went from Bancroft to the Madoc area to visit his relatives.

Now, some 40 years later, we have fond memories of those trips on which we took along a snack of his Mom's homemade taffy tarts and a thermos of tea. In those days the golden arches of Macdonalds were unheard of. A roadside park, our picnic snack, and close proximity in the front seat of this '41 Chev made these trips extra-special. Yes, I married 'the driver' and we have owned many cars since, but none have had quite the same appeal as that '41 Chev with the hole in the floor.

Mealtime Panic

Dad, like myself, had to eat at regular times, never longer than five hours between meals. When I was a kid we thought this was just a fetish of his. As I grew, however, I found that I would become weak if I went longer than that without food. Dad never complained of weakness but he would be pretty agitated if his meals weren't ready.

The family still laughs at Mom's ploy if she was a little late having the meal ready. "Set the table, Heather. If the table is set your Dad will think the meal is ready." It always worked. Dad would sit down at the table and, contentedly, eat bread and butter with pickles while he waited for the main course and never complained or questioned the strategy.

Beets to Beat All

Fast-food in my childhood days had a whole different concept than today. All meals were made by Mom in the kitchen at home. The fast-food idea then was 'how can we speed up the cooking' and the answer was "the pressure cooker" ! It was a far cry from the microwave cooking of today but, for the harried housewife, it was fast.

I still see pressure cookers for sale today. The newer versions are in the stores. The older models are at auction sales. They older ones are heavy stainless steel cooking pots with wooden handles and a gauge on the lid. Once the ingredients are in the pot it is extremely important that this lid be screwed on tightly. After all, the contents are to be cooked under pressure.

The most graphic recollection of the power of the pressure cooker is the day my mother cooked beets. We brought them from the garden, washed them, cut the tops off and into the pressure cooker they went. We had acquired an electric range, another work-saving device, and Mom popped the cooker on a red-hot element and then went scurrying about to get the rest of the meal together. I was at my post at the telephone switchboard but in no time at all I heard the pressure-gauge screaming. I knew the beets were finished and it was just a matter of letting the pot cool so that it was safe to take off the lid.

Several minutes later I was jolted from my chair by more screaming, not from the pressure-gauge this time but from my mother. I was in the kitchen instantly and, relieved to see my mother standing intact, I followed her gaze to the ceiling above the range. Such wonderful abstract design I had never seen! There was ruby-coloured beet juice everywhere. What had been a freshly- painted, white ceiling was nothing less than a nightmare. I didn't know whether to laugh or cry. In a stupor I asked, "What happened?"

"I didn't check the gauge and I guess I took the lid off too soon. What a mess," she said as she shook her head and sighed.

I had to agree with that. Right then the atmosphere was a bit like a pressure cooker. Mom needed lots of time and space to cool. That was definitely one time that I was glad that Mom valued my skills as a telephone operator more than she did my help in the kitchen. After a very subdued lunch I was sent back to my telephone post so that Mom could clean off the art work undisturbed. I don't think beets were ever on her list of favourite vegetables after that.

Heather's Schooling

The old grades 1&2 room now used by Rainbow Club

It began in 1947 in a three-room frame school about a ten minute walk from our house. The " grades one and two room" of that school remains and is on the same site as in 1947. For the last few years it has housed the seniors' "Rainbow Club". In 1949 we pupils all helped move to the "new school", which still forms the basis of the present school.

My first teacher was Shirley Turner, the former Shirley Gunter, daughter of Dick and Laura Gunter and, therefore, my cousin. The principal was Gertie Gunter who was extremely short in stature but very much "in charge". In reminiscing just recently with Marjorie (Peacock) Painter, I learned that Gertie had to stand on a chair in order to reach the older children if she had to strap them! Take a moment just to picture that!

I don't recall too much about the first few years except that I had a tendency to use the eraser end more than the lead end of the pencil! I either made a lot of mistakes or I kept changing my mind.

I do recall the first readers. Who can forget Dick, Jane, Sally, Spot and Puff? Who could forget that stimulating dialogue: "Oh look, Jane. See Spot run. See Puff run. See Spot and Puff run!"

Not a farm girl, but raised in a farming community, I can close my eyes even now and see on the classroom wall the large framed pictures of each popular breed of cow and of work-horse. Today, picking out Red Angus, Shorthorn and Herefords as we drive past the beef farms is no problem, but what are these Limousins, Charolais and Simmentals? Obviously there has been a change in traditional farming over the forty-some years since I received my bit of agricultural training.

Being able to name on sight each wild flower, each weed and most of the birds in Ontario was a much-enjoyed part of the natural science taught to us in elementary school. Sadly, very little of that is on today's curriculum.

I did well in the beginning years at school and so I think Mrs. Turner was an excellent teacher. It's strange though that the thing that sticks in my mind all these years is not any lesson or game. Instead it is seeing Mrs. Turner walking up and down the aisle with her finger pressed to one nostril and a Vick's Inhaler held to the other nostril as she inhaled. I suppose that was

Grades 3,4,5 at Coe Hill Public School, Oct.1948

Back Row: Miss Narduzzi, Gail Forbes, Marlene Hannah, Beatrice Unger, Marjorie Tivy, Bernice Vader, Faye Marshal, Marjorie Peacock, Colleen Wilson, Heather Gunter, Diane Post
Middle Row: Jean Marshal, Wilma McCaw, Belvia Unger, Colleen Campbell, Rhoda Finnegan, Winnie Davidson, Emily Bird, Amy Wannamker, Shirley Unger, Patty Landon, Nello Foran
Front Row: Melvern Woodbeck, Graydon Campbell, Vernon Ferguson, Lyman Landon, Allan Baumhour, 'Buster'Landon, Murray Crosby, Charlie Finnegan, Doug Martin, Trevor Whitmore

the first I'd seen this medicinal wonder and I was fascinated with it. I've bought many for myself since and I'm sure I think of her each time.

By grade 2 or 3 the new brick school was finished and we all moved there. In the elementary years remaining, I had a series of teachers: Miss Henderson, Miss Narduzzi, Mr. Foreacre, Mr. Johnson and Bert Giles. Much credit goes to Bert for taking over mid-year and getting our grade eight class ready for high school. In those years, and still today, Coe Hill students were bussed to North Hastings High School at Bancroft.

Additional classrooms have been added over the years and in 1983, long after my schooling, a gymnasium was added for which I am sure today's teachers and students are so grateful.

Bosom Buddies

Neighbour Marjorie Tivy and I

Allyn and Reg Tivy with Tivy house in background.

In a small town everyone is like family. You have many good friends. I think back with fondness to such people as Marjorie Tivy, my very first friend and closest neighbour, to Heather Graham who taught me to skip double-dutch, to Norman Lehigh who was so gracious with his car, and to Jim Sharp who taught me so much about driving. These are a few of many. Of those good friends, especially during your elementary school days, one often becomes special. For me it was Wilma McCaw, now Wilma Crosby, married to Murray. Although we did branch out and form other close and lasting friendships in high school, we started school together and finished together, both of us even becoming teachers. While we were in elementary school we shared many hours of play and togetherness. We swam together at Eagle Lake Beach (now Wollaston Lake), we picked pussy willows in the spring along the road to the lake and we sang together in choirs and engaged in friendly vocal competition at the Kiwanis Music Festival in Bancroft (I think Wilma usually won).

Wilma McCaw and I. In the background is the old "Company House" that Mom and Dad lived in when first married and where Dad first had his bakery.

Birthdays were always a big event. I can remember attending one of Wilma's January birthday parties. Her mom, Pearl, was a wonderful cook and the cake was absolutely delicious. Of course, as was the custom then, prizes were hidden in the cake. I'm not sure if it was because of the taste of the cake or the hoping to get a prize (I suspect it was the latter), but I had at least four pieces of cake, more than I could possibly handle comfortably. Shortly after I got home I was very sick, and I knew why. I'm sure I was an embarrassment to my mother when she learned of my lack of manners.

Another thing that stands out vividly in my mind is

"our playhouse". It was the camper part of a camping van that was parked behind Bill's (Wilma's Dad) garage. With cupboards, sink, and bunks, it was the perfect playhouse. But we were at that inquisitive age too, about 11 or 12 I think. If my mother reads this I expect it will be a shocking revelation to her, but Wilma and I tried our first smokes there. We helped ourselves to her Dad's supply of loose tobacco and cigarette papers and we actually rolled our own! When we ran out of tobacco we improvised with grass (from the lawn, not today's grass!). The taste wasn't great and the smell was worse. Maybe that is why the whole thing didn't appeal to us much and we gave it up after a couple of days. My teenage grandkids were horrified when I recently confessed this story to them. I guess they just can't picture me puffing on a cigarette, not to mention rolling my own!

Kindred Spirits

Childhood recollections would never be complete without mentioning Frank and Hilda Sprackett and their family, namely, Terry, Donna, Jeanne, and Bill. Besides being close family friends, they owned the store in the center of town, just over the hill from us. This store at one time had been owned by Kingerleys, and before that it was owned by Walkers, the grandparents of Vivian (now Mrs. Garnet Gunter) and Verda(now Mrs. Andy Campbell). Spracketts had lived in

Jeanne & Donna Sprackett

Ormsby until 1950. Their Ormsby house burnt in November of 1948, leaving them with only a garage. Hilda had been away supply teaching and Frank had been ploughing so they lost almost everything, including the already-purchased Christmas gifts. As Donna says, "It was a pretty slim Christmas."

To make living accommodations, they finished the upstairs part of the garage and lived there for awhile. In 1950 they opted to buy the store in Coe Hill and move into the living quarters which came with the store. This store was a forerunner of today's convenience store. You could buy the basic canned goods and nonperishables there as well as candy, pop, and ice-cream. There was also a Tea Room.

In front of Sprackett's Store:
Jeanne Sprackett, Anne Giles, Kay Giles, Lois Whitmore, Judy Whitmore
(Probably early 1950's)

In addition, Hilda opened up a line of clothing that was displayed along one wall of the tearoom. My most vivid memory of shopping there is buying a pink cotton dirndl skirt for $2.50 as my new outfit to start school in the sixth grade. Usually Mom made my clothes, but for some reason she bought me that skirt. In fact, I don't remember too many home-sewn clothes after grade six. I suppose I had reached that hard-to-please age.

Mom still has the set of dishes that she acquired from Sprackett's store . For a predetermined number of dollars spent on groceries, you earned a

Hilda and Donna pouring tea at Mom and Dad's 50th anniversary

plate, or a cup or whatever the weekly premium was. Eventually there was a chance to buy any pieces you were missing to finish out the set. The pattern is much like the Royal Doulton "cottage rose", but the china is not quite as fine; however, it means as much or more to us.

I have a mantel-type clock that I won at Christmas on a punch-board at Sprackett's store. As I recall, you punched a name on the board and when you tore off that name, the amount you paid was underneath. I think I paid 50 cents. When all the names had been purchased, the winner was revealed. I had chosen the name Maria because someone had told me that usually old names win. I thought that was close to my Grandmother Soble's name. Her name was pronounced Mar-eye-a but it was spelled Maria. The clock is a goldplated horse on a plastic base with a clockface mounted separately beside it. I think it is a replica of a much more expensive one that I saw recently at an antique show.

The little store was eventually remodeled while Spracketts had it and it became a two-storey building that housed a restaurant and much bigger living quarters for the family. They also rented out rooms to overnight travelers and would take in boarders too. I can recall hydro workers staying there in 1950 when hydro was being introduced to Coe Hill.

Hilda eventually quit selling clothes but, for a couple of years, I was fortunate to be the recipient of many of Donna's hand-me-down clothes. She was a year older than I so it worked out fine.

Our families shared many other things too. Hilda and Mom knew each other's tastes so well that they could actually buy hats for each other since they weren't always able to go to the city together. Wearing a hat to church and all formal functions was a must in the 50's.

I think each of Terry, Donna, Jeanne, and Bill learned to operate our telephone switchboard. I liked to have company at my otherwise lonely post. It was also good to have a relief- worker.

Our two families often went on Sunday trips together, usually to Algonquin Park with a picnic lunch. In later years, when we kids were older, our parents camped and traveled on more extensive trips together, without us, of course. They loved to play euchre and often got together in the evening for this, the men against the women.

Dad & Mom with the Spracketts at Agawa Canyon.

Music was another common interest for Frank and Howard, and this love of music was passed to us all. Dad played the piano and the guitar. Frank played the violin. Terry eventually played the piano too. Sometimes we had a practice-session in our living room. Both men also sang in the church choir and, in time, we kids did too. We all loved to sing and still do.

Dad and Frank Sprackett sharing some music

Music Lessons

Dad and Mom either felt I had some musical aptitude or hoped it would blossom. Maybe they just got tired of hearing me trying out the old pump organ at Grandma Gunter's. At any rate, when Frank Whitely, not only a minister but also a pianist, arrived in town, the opportunity for lessons presented itself. I was only seven at the time. I don't think Rev. Whitely had ever taught piano lessons before but he was willing to try, refusing to accept any money for it. Some of my first pieces were hymns such as "When He Cometh" and "Jesus Loves Me". Mom and Dad had purchased a used piano from the Kingerley family for me.

Unfortunately, as ministers do, Rev. Whitely moved after I had had a year or two of lessons. After that I had a series of teachers, namely Phyllis Giles (Tiny), Ralph MacDonald, Marguerite Ingram, and Adrian Schmidt. Each one in turn had a different strength, and the changes were probably good for me. Taking lessons from Marguerite is the most remembered by me, so I think I was with her the longest. I do know that she was (and is) a stickler for having the correct beat. If the piece is written with four beats to the bar, then you'd better have that many, no more and no less! I can remember sitting at her piano, with tears streaming down my face, glad that she was standing behind me and could not see. She, meanwhile, was tapping out the beat with a pencil, and calling out, "One, two, three, four, one two, three, four." I was having quite a challenge to keep up with her and play the right notes at the same time. I'm sure she sensed my frustration but was wise enough not to acknowledge it.

At home, Dad insisted I play by note, not by ear, and Mom, although she had had no lessons, knew the

Practice-time for members of the United Church Choir with Tiny Giles as organist (1940's): Howard Gunter, Marguerite Hanthorn, Tom Hanthorn, Dick Gunter

value of repetition and made sure that I did my daily practicing. I thank her now, and all those along the way who helped me. Not only was I church organist as a teenager, but I have used my piano skills in my classroom teaching, in community endeavors, and for my own enjoyment. Today in retirement I am even teaching piano. Being able to read music has added so much to my life and, hopefully, through my music, I have helped to bring enjoyment to others.

Indelibly Etched

It hung on the dining room wall all the years I was growing up. The plaque was about a foot and a half wide and made of some type of black glass. There was a fine gold line border. The words printed on it were in white. Mom says she has no idea who gave it to her, nor what happened to it after they moved from that house to the stone house at the west end of the village. It doesn't really matter because the words are forever etched in my mind: "There is so much bad in the best of us and so much good in the worst of us, that it hardly behooves any of us to talk about the rest of us." What a wonderful bit of philosophy!

Another bit of philosophy that wasn't hung on the wall but quoted enough times by Dad that it too became indelibly etched is: "If you are not enjoying life, it could be the fault of the liver". I was young when I first heard that one and I didn't really get the full significance of it until later, learning it was akin to " A person is as happy as he makes up his mind to be".

Allyn often uses another quote of Dad's when he is pleased with something: "Number One Copper Bottom". Frank explained to us all just recently what he thought to be the origin of that. In good cooking pots the best grade of copper is used on the bottom.

Must All Girls Have Curls?

Me with curls from rags

My cousin Sandra had beautifully curly hair. Friends Donna and Jeanne had natural curls. My friend Wilma had natural waves. I, on the other hand, had a thick mane of stubborn, straight brown hair. From about grade two to grade six, Mom braided it in precise French braids, not a hair allowed to jump out of place. On the occasion of weddings or parties though, curls were in order. Mom would section off strand upon strand of wet hair and wind it on white rags, knotted to stay in place all night. The rags were removed in the morning, and I would have curls for the day.

By the time I was eleven or twelve 'home perms'

had become the rage, literally a permanent hair-do that could be done at home by the amateur. Mom bought the brand called "Toni". The box contained the waving solution, the neutralizer, the plastic perm rods, and the directions. After an afternoon session with this, the house as well as my hair smelled horrid, but I had curls! Frizz would better describe it. The hair was tightly kinked and, because I had such thick hair, it stuck out all over. I had to endure that for a week or so. Each shampooing loosened it up a bit and in time my hair might pass for curly. That would last about three or four months and then it was time to do it again. Each time Mom would reduce the number of minutes that the solution was left on my hair so that maybe the "frizzies" would not be as bad as the time before. When I look at the photos taken in those Toni-days, I have a tendency to turn the page quickly. I think I rejoiced when the "ducktail" became the popular haircut. It was perfect for straight hair and I wore that style for most of my high school days.

Me with my ducktail hairstyle about 1956

Chapter Seventeen

Life in The Political Ring

Dad's initiation into local politics would certainly prove that "nothing is stranger than people", and perhaps uphold that "truth is stranger than fiction". Dad first became part of the Coe Hill council without even having to let his name stand for an election. A councillor had quit and Clarke Rollins, who was reeve at the time, came to the house to talk Dad into finishing out the term until the next election. Dad was not overly anxious to take on this position, but Clarke was very persuasive. Finally Dad consented, but then at the very first meeting Clarke wanted Dad to make a motion to have an employee fired. Dad was not in favour of that because, in his opinion, this man was doing a good job and it would be a hardship to everyone concerned. Dad refused to make the motion and Clarke reacted! He indicated that from now on Howard Gunter would be the acting reeve. He stormed out of the council chambers and never came back for a meeting. Dad finished out the term as reeve.

Neither Dad nor his secretary had had any experience in the striking of the levy. How did they manage? Dad said that they simply looked at last year's figures and they knew that the commercial levy was higher than the general. "We did know a little arithmetic too, you know," Dad chuckled, "and so we took the overall amount of the assessments and struck the general levy and then just made the commercial a little higher. Somehow, with the council's help, we made it through the year."

Dad continued as councillor in the next election, but didn't try for reeveship until years later.

Reeve By Election

Yes, beginning in 1980, Dad's name appeared on the voter's ballot as a candidate for reeve. He was voted in that year, and continued serving in that capacity until 1988. He definitely was not a speechmaker, but he did have a genuine interest in seeing Coe Hill maintain its standards and prosper if possible. He could talk to anyone on a one-to-one basis. For the most part he was able to keep a level head, although he did chew a lot of Rolaid tablets in those years of being reeve!

He felt success at times and disappointments at other times. 'Life Leathercraft Company' was both. A newcomer to the area by the name of Tom Spadafore in 1975 had started a small cottage industry in Coe Hill that made leather crafts such as hats, belts, and souvenirs. In the spring of 1980 it employed 100 area people and business was booming. That May they moved into a new $500,000 plant with better equipment. By 1981 the company had run into financial difficulty made worse by a lengthy mail strike. Dad and council were supportive in Tom's request to all branches of government for assistance to keep this industry alive in Coe Hill, but to no avail. The business venture was terminated and many dreams of employment and better financial times for the area were dashed. A recent enquiry I made confirmed that Tom Spadafore is still living in Coe Hill and doing some crafts in his own house, but the factory itself is silent.

A request by the Wollaston Council of 1981 to the Neighbourhood Improvement Fund resulted in enough financial help to permit an addition being added to the eastern side of the school in 1983. This addition doubled as a school gymnasium and a Community Centre. Its official opening in May of 1984 was one of the proud moments in Dad's life, the lives of the council members who had initiated this effort, and the

1949 School

Present School.

lives of all Wollaston residents.

Dad retired from Municipal Politics in 1988 after eight years of continuous service as Reeve of Wollaston Township. In a surprise presentation at the last council meeting he received an engraved gold watch from the council, the office staff, the road crew, the recreation committee, the fire department and its auxiliary. Usually not a sentimental man, he was touched by this gesture.

Although he was finished serving, his interest in politics, whether federal, provincial, or municipal, continued as long as he lived. It was a subject he loved to discuss.

I soon came to know that there was no sense moaning to Dad about how much income tax I'd had to pay. "Heather," he would say, "You know you must have made the money or you wouldn't have had to pay taxes on it."

As more and more accusations of government scandal and corruption surface these days, I sometimes think that it's a good thing Dad did not live to witness these things. The steadfast faith he seemed to have in our country's government would have been severely tested.

Dad's last council meeting Dec 4, 1988
Back: Councillors Norm Conlin, Rob Henderson, Doris Danford, Albert Vader
Front: Betty Wilson(clerk), Dad, Geraldine Woodbeck (assistant clerk)

Chapter Eighteen

Entrepreneuring To Benefit Others

Dad kept trying to come up with an industry for Coe Hill, a vision on which he never gave up. Although he didn't smoke, I guess he thought there was an industrial future in growing tobacco. I was probably 17 or 18 when Dad and Mom made a trip to southern Ontario and they observed the fields of tobacco and the kilns, asking questions about the growth, the curing, etc. Dad realized it was a very sandy soil, not unlike the Coe Hill area.

The next year he made his first attempt at tobacco farming, sowing the seeds in early spring. The seeds grew tall, high over Dad's head. At harvest time he cured their large leaves in the garage, which he said was a bit of a task, but he didn't have access to a kiln. Many people were interested and asked lots of questions but that's as far as it seemed to go. No one, including Dad, went any further with the idea. I still think it ironic that Dad, who found the whole idea of tobacco-smoking so repulsive, would even consider trying to grow tobacco.

The tobacco-growing experiment had been a learning-experience in more ways than one. During the plowing session, Dad's wallet which contained forty or fifty dollars had been lost and no amount of searching uncovered it. Not that year anyway. But six years later, while that same land was being tilled, up popped the wallet! Dad, anxious to show Mom, hurried to the house with it. Naturally , they opened it up to look at the money. To their chagrin, the bills simply disintegrated the moment they made contact with the air. Too late they learned that they should have sent the wallet intact to Ottawa and the bills could have been viewed by some special process and replaced. Now how many people would have known that?

Dad also completed the first steps for starting a co-op in Coe Hill and area. The focus was to be on growing

Dad and Grandson Christopher Gunter getting ready for potato planting in 1985, only as a hobby now.

potatoes, and people from as far away as Palmer Rapids came to the meetings. Ivan Gunter, and Gene Lockart were two local people who grew potatoes. The crops were a success and the whole idea was good until the potato-price took a sudden dive to 50 cents a bushel. No one could afford to grow them. Dad had had a huge patch on Aunt Madge's property. Dave Wannamaker sold all he could for Dad through the store and Dad had to dump the rest. He lost on this venture.

Clair Canfield , a local resident, and Ivan shared the cost of some big equipment for potato growing. They chose a beautiful smooth potato as their first venture. It turned out to be a slow-growing variety and that year they lost money because of early frost. Gene Lockart and Ivan apparently did continue potato growing but the co-op never developed.

Dad said that both tobacco and potatoes grow well in Coe Hill's climate and sandy soil. Either one could probably be a success as long as the market remained stable.

In a separate operation, that of trying to make maple syrup, Dad said he squandered at least a thousand dollars. The sap ran well and he had bought plastic tubing to run from tree to tree. The unfortunate part was that because he was busy and couldn't stay at the site keeping a watch on things, the squirrels chewed holes in the tubing. Today there are better methods. Reverse osmosis has been a success. Coe Hill could probably produce more syrup than it does. Dad remarked about how quickly maples grow there and that it was a natural place for maple syrup production.

Frank still laughs appreciatively at the memory of some of Dad's original inventions. One of these was Dad's sap reservoir. Dad, although an avid fisherman, had no qualms about having his aluminum boat do double-duty. There it sat in the bush, three plastic hoses of sap feeding into it. This precious but sticky sap was siphoned out the other end of the boat and into the boiling pan in the sugar shack. At the close of maple-syrup season he simply washed out his boat and returned it to the storage shed until it was time for fishing season!

I do remember one time that Dad convinced Mom that it would be no trouble to boil the last bit of sap in the kitchen at the house. As anyone knows, it takes a lot of sap to make a little syrup, so it was a long session of boiling and the resulting stickiness of that evaporation was evident in our kitchen until the next good cleaning and painting. Dad knew better than to ever suggest in-the-kitchen syrup making again.

If Dad was ever discouraged about his visions not working out, he didn't let it show. His guiding philosophy in everything in life seemed to be: Don't push, if it's to be, it will be. In the words of the song, "Que Sera, Sera".

With Mom's support he tried many different ventures in life, and at 86 summed it up with, "I didn't really go out looking for new things. They just came my way and, with your mother's help, I bumbled from one thing to another."

As I sat beside Dad's bed in the hospital the day before he died in 1997, I reminded him that he had had a good life. He was strangely silent. I think there were still so many things he would like to have tried. The spirit was still willing but the flesh was weak.

Chapter Nineteen

Final Words

I have often heard the expression "a labour of love". The writing of these memories and the searching through photo albums has been just that. The task has consumed many hours of both concentrated and sporadic efforts over the past four years. The editing and the polishing, those finishing touches, have been the biggest challenge.

It did "take me home". We can't live in the past, but it's gratifying to visit there now and then. My sincere hope is that all my readers found interest in the stories and the history.

This book has focused on "my roots". There are many more stories to tell involving "the branching out". I'll save them for another day.

This is how the show has gone on :

Frank & Heather Campbell

Allyn & Maureen (Leveque)
Gunter

Son Kevin, Heather, Frank,
Laurie (Campbell)Gervais

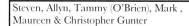

Steven, Allyn, Tammy (O'Brien), Mark ,
Maureen & Christopher Gunter

Campbell / Gervais Wedding

Laurie on her Wedding Day
Aug. 8,1987

The Gunter and Campbell Clan
Aug. 8,1987

The Granddaughters

2002

Left : Amanda Gervais
14 Yrs

Right: Jessica Gervais
13 yrs

Hazel with L. to R.
Jessica, Laurie,
Amanda Gervais
and their ceramic
doll collection

Dad, one of the last Coe Hill years, with great- granddaughters Amanda and Jessica.

Perry ~ Campbell Wedding

Kevin Campbell and Kimberley Perry on their Aug 29,1998 Wedding Day

The Campbells and the Gunters on Aug. 29, 1998

The Gunter Name Continues

Paige Rankin, Steven Gunter,
Tammy (O'Brien) & Mark Gunter

The Combined Gunter & Campbell Families May 29, 1999

The Gunter Name Continues

Christopher Gunter

Tammy, Mark & Sam Gunter

Latest Feature Starring:

Sam Allyn Gunter, born Feb. 20, 2002

Four Generations of Gunters: Allyn, Hazel, Sam, and Mark

Other Readings

1. **Touring**
     by Bob Lyons   1987
  Published by Northern Source Books,
          Bancroft, Ont.

2. **Joe Alcorn's Boy**
   by William D. Hanthorn
   1981   Madoc Printing and Publishing

3. **McClure Heritage**
  by Darius King Card 1966
   Picton Gazette Publishing Company

4. **I Remember Grandma**
   Copyright 1993 by Annie Faul and Patricia
   Husak

5. **It's Not All Roses**
   The Autobiography of Rev.Leslie J. Hardy 1985
 (Quad Printing)

6. **A Brief History of Wollaston Township**
   Copyright by A.G. Giles
   March 9, 1953

ISBN 155395794-6